KidLit-O Presents

What's So Great About Mozart?
A Biography of Wolfgang Amadeus Mozart Just For Kids

Max Tanner

KidLit-O Books
www.kidlito.com

Table of Contents

About KidCaps
Introduction
Chapter 1: Early Life and Childhood Tours
Chapter 2: When in Rome
Chapter 3: Mozart Roams Europe
Chapter 4: The Return to Vienna
Chapter 5: Uphill and Downhill
Chapter 6: Money Troubles
Chapter 7: The Death and Legacy of Mozart

About KidCaps

KidLit-O is an imprint of BookCaps™ that is just for kids! Each month BookCaps will be releasing several books in this exciting imprint. Visit are website or like us on Facebook to see more!

To add your name to our mailing list, visit this link: http://www.kidlito.com/mailing-list.html

Introduction

His name is one of the most recognizable in the history of classical music. He learned much from the musicians that came before him, and he inspired generations of musicians after him. His work with the piano and strings was revolutionary at the time, and it continues to stun and amaze people today. You could listen to hours of his music, and still only scrape the tip of the iceberg.

His name was Wolfgang Amadeus Mozart, and he was fated to go down as one of history's greatest musical innovators. He grew up in a world in which music was changing, and he joined the musical revolution. Mozart was called a genius during his life, and he is still called a genius by many today. But why? What did he do that was so great? If anyone can learn to write music, what made his music so special? Why will Mozart be remembered for centuries to come? Here we will explore Mozart's life and what it meant to the world.

Chapter 1: Early Life and Childhood Tours

In the year 1737, a man named Leopold Mozart moved from the town of Augsburg, Austria to the town of Salzburg. As an eighteen-year old musician, Leopold was having a hard time finding good audiences. He was a good player overall, but the world was full of good players, and he just needed the right moment to find the right spot for him. It took him ten years to get to where he wanted to be; by the end of the decade, he was composing music for the Salzburg court (where all the royalty spent their time!), and even conducting orchestras as well.

During his musical adventures, he met a beautiful girl named Anna Maria Bertl, who had lived in Salzburg for much longer than Leopold had. The two of them fell in love and married; little did they know they would have a child that would reshape the world as they knew it.

Leopold and Anna were very excited to have children. Now that Leopold was an established musician with a steady income, he would be able to support his family. However, not many of their children survived. During this time period, it was very rare for all the children in a family to survive very long. In general, things were not as sanitary as they are today. Many people got diseases and lived short lives; today, though, we have medicines and technology that can help us avoid such misfortunes.

Leopold and Anna were not so lucky. They had seven children in total, but only two of them survived. One of them, the oldest, they named Marianne (although they nicknamed her Nannerl, and called her this). The other was named Johannes Chrysostomus Wolfgangus Theophilus Mozart—the person who we all now know as Wolfgang Amadeus Mozart. Many people during this time had two names: there was the one that they were baptized with, and the ones that they liked to be referred by. Mozart much preferred "Wolfgang Amadeus" than his much longer name.

From the moment that baby Wolfgang saw the light of day on January 27th, 1756 he was listening to his music. The Mozart family often dined with rich guests who had musicians play for them during mealtime, and besides that, Leopold Mozart loved to play for his family. With such an environment growing up, it was hard for baby Wolfgang *not* to be interested in music—especially when he was taught to play the piano at the age of four.

Scientists often say that the best time to learn an instrument is when you're young. Before you become an adult, your brain is still trying to learn everything that is possibly can as quickly as possible. It has been proved that you are more likely to become proficient at an instrument if you start as a child rather than later—also, you have more time to work at it!

Many famous musicians were not only born into musical households, but also started learning instruments around the age of four. Mozart was no exception to this. His father

Leopold loved teaching his child how to play the piano. Sometimes he would cry and pout until his father taught his how to play certain songs on the piano; one thing is for sure, and it is that Mozart was desperate to learn more.

But some people say that Mozart's upbringing was not the only reason he became famous. Some people say that he was born with a special talent that made him stand out. For instance, sometimes he could just listen to a piece of music and then instantly play it without looking at the notes. He usually did not need to be taught anything more than once.

Other people say that neither Mozart's nature nor his environment were the reason for his popularity. Some claim that his father, as a musician, was the best teacher. He made his son practice for a certain amount of time each day. This did not always include playing music. Sometimes he would sit and copy down music composed by other famous musicians, so that he would have to focus on every little note as he drew it. This plays a very important part in how we learn instruments: practice every day, no matter what. As the saying goes, "It is better to practice for fifteen minutes each day, than one hour every three days."

This practice obviously paid off. By the time that he was five years old, Mozart had already written his first piece of music. It was a *minuet*, which is a slow dance. In the same year, he played for his first audience, a piece of music from an opera. When the audience saw the five-year old child playing advanced music, they knew that they were seeing something special. Leopold Mozart, of all people, was incredibly proud.

He knew that he would have to show Mozart off to the world. He told a group of friends that "It is my duty to convince the world of this miracle, especially nowadays when people scoff and deny all miracles." From that moment, Leopold knew that his son would become something great, and he wanted to be there for his son every step of the way.

Today, celebrities have agents. The agents arrange interviews and performances, how the celebrity gets from place to place, who they talk to, and they spread word of the celebrity in order to increase popularity and fame. Mozart did not have an agent; he only had his father Leopold. He told everyone he knew about his genius son. But if he *really* wanted his son to make his impression, he knew they would have to travel to Vienna, the capital of Austria, where they could play for the royal court.

The royals of the Viennese court knew that Mozart was coming, and they were excited. People around the country had been talking about Mozart for a couple of years; now, they wanted to see the child prodigy! When Leopold and Mozart arrived, they were introduced to Empress Maria Theresa, the ruler of Austria.

When the child Mozart saw the Empress, he sat on her lap and kissed her cheek. Everyone thought this was absolutely adorable (and people still wonder to this day whether Leopold told his son to do this, or whether it was entirely Mozart's own doing).

The whole royal family was astounded when Mozart started playing, especially the Empress. It was certainly a sight to behold.

Leopold and Mozart stayed in Vienna for quite some time. Mozart loved spending time with the other children in the palace; the Empress's daughters made for great company. It was here in Vienna that Mozart met Marie Antoinette, a very famous historical figure.

Marie Antoinette was one of Empress Maria Theresa's daughters. Later in her life, she married a man of French royalty named Louis-Auguste. While the French people liked her at first, they soon suspected her of playing favorites with France's enemies, particularly Austria, the country where she was born and where she met Mozart. She tended to spend too much money while the French people were starving, she had romantic affairs with other men, and eventually the French people could not take it any more. The whole French royal family was imprisoned; she was put to trial, and convicted of treason against the country of France. In 1793, when she was thirty-seven years old, she was executed.

Wolfgang Amadeus Mozart always thought that he might marry Marie Antoinette one day, but after her move to Paris, France, it never happened.

Leopold and Mozart did not only stay in the Viennese palace. Wealthy aristocrats across Vienna wanted to hear the young boy play. But as the weeks wore on, so too did Leopold's money. There was a spell of time during their tour that Mozart became ill due to so many performances, and no one wanted to go near the boy for fear of catching the sickness. Back home, the Archbishop of Salzburg was infuriated with Leopold for being away so long; Leopold was supposed to be playing and composing music for him.

Leopold decided that their tour of Vienna would have to come to an end. Despite the fact that he wanted to stay, he realized that, for his son, this was the start of something grand that would change their lives forever.

But no matter how aggravated the Archbishop of Salzburg may have been, Leopold knew that he and his son *needed* to travel once again. After all, many people only wanted to see Mozart for his young age. That was what made him spectacular (for now, at least). They just could not wait any longer. But where were they to go next? Leopold decided that Paris, France would be their best bet. It was a city of wealth and art and music. Yes, he was sure they would do great there.

Their trip to Paris took six months, because Leopold insisted that they stop in several cities along the way. Essentially, he wanted to stop anywhere that Mozart could play for some money. Young Mozart became sick on the way. He was not yet twelve years old, and he was already bracing the extreme weather of the German countryside. Some days it was freezing cold, windy and rainy, and the next it was unbearably hot. They stayed at inns that were not very sanitary, and Mozart ended up sick once again. But his father Leopold insisted that they continue their journey.

Once they arrived in Paris, Leopold was not exactly sure how to gain the attention of the French royal family. One man, however, helped them through the difficult situation. His name was Friedrich Melchior Grimm, a German writer and musician who held much respect in Parisian society. He published an article in a magazine, announcing that the young Wolfgang Amadeus Mozart had arrived in Paris with his father Leopold, and that everyone should see the prodigy! Grimm communicated with many aristocrats and set up performances; if not for Grimm, Mozart might never have had a proper audience during his stay in Paris.

People adored Mozart's playing, but Mozart could not say the same for the people of Paris. While he loved the city, both he and his father shared contempt for French music. They thought the music was boring and monotonous, but that did not stop him from enjoying the city and the royal family. Mozart and Leopold even got to spend their time with the Queen of Paris and the rest of the royal family on New Year's Day.

While Mozart and Leopold stayed in Paris, Mozart wrote two pieces of music. They were two *sonatas*, for the violin and piano. A *sonata* is a song with more than one section, or *movement*, which is usually played by one instrument and accompanied by another. In this case, the violin was the prominent instrument, and the piano was the accompaniment. Even at such a young age, his talent was growing, and the audiences of Paris wanted more and more of it.

Leopold, however, saw the great opportunity to travel somewhere else. Now that his son's name had spread across France, he wanted the Mozart name to visit elsewhere. Mozart and his father traveled to London, England. When they arrived in the city, they were immediately taken to the royal palace, to see King George III and Queen Charlotte.

Both the king and queen loved music and often listened to concerts (since they were king and queen, they could hear just about anything they wanted to!). The whole royal court loved hearing Mozart play and, as in Vienna and Paris, Mozart played for wealthy aristocrats in addition to the royal family.

It was here in London that Mozart met yet another important historical figure: Johann Christian Bach. Johann Christian's father was Johann Sebastian Bach, one of the most influential musicians of all time. In London, Johann Christian served as the Queen of England's personal Music Master, playing for her and even composing music. His father, Johann Sebastian, had inspired numerous other musical celebrities, and continues to even today. The musician Chopin said that Bach had every single thing perfect, and that every one of his notes was so brilliantly written that to change any one of them would be a tragedy. While Johann Christian never filled the big shoes of his father, he still lived a successful life in England. He also enjoyed young Mozart's playing.

Later in his life, Mozart said that Johann Christian taught him much about music, especially Italian music. Because of Johann Christian, Mozart started to explore operas and even got the opportunity to meet Giovanni Manzuoli, a famous Italian opera singer. Despite the fact that he was now determined to work on an opera piece, Mozart decided he would write a symphony, a large collection of both horn instruments (trumpets, clarinets, and so on) and string instruments (violins, cellos, et cetera).

While the eight-year old Mozart was certainly making musical progress at the time, many historians and scholars criticize Leopold's treatment of his children. For such a young child, so many performances and such a busy schedule was harmful to Mozart's health. Even Nannerl, who had been traveling with them, fell ill. On one hand, people say that Leopold only wanted his children to be successful, and for the Mozart name to be famous; after all, he risked his job in Salzburg so that he could travel with his son and daughter. On the other hand, he risked the health of his children with such a hectic few years. Mozart continued to get sick, but Leopold always wanted to push onwards.

When Leopold learned that the Archbishop of Salzburg would no longer pay him for his absence, Leopold shrugged it off and decided that their next destination would be Italy.

Chapter 2: When in Rome

The Mozart family first visited the city of Verona, the famed city of Shakespeare's *Romeo and Juliet*. After that, they found themselves in the city of Milan and then Rome. It was here in Rome that Mozart did something that many musicians and historians still talk about today.

In the Sistine Chapel, the church's organist would play a song called *Miserere* by Gregorio Allegri. The song is allegedly so beautiful and so sacred that, at the time, no one else was allowed to play it. Members of the Sistine Chapel were not allowed to copy down the music, or to remove the sheet music from the church. Anyone that was caught trying to sneak the music out or memorize it was immediately disbanded from the Church—something that was looked down upon in Rome.

Leopold, however, wanted to take the risk. He asked Mozart to remember the song and write it all down. And Mozart did. He had to listen to *Miserere* twice in order to get all the notes right, but at such a young age, he was able to write down sheet music simply by listening to it.

The Sistine Chapel found out. But instead of excommunicating him, or expelling him from the church, the church was amazed that a boy could accomplish all of that. A man named Count Pallavicini even decided to support the Mozart family during their time in Italy, giving them shelter and incredible opportunities for sightseeing in the city of Naples.

The people of Italy also adored Mozart's music, almost more than any other location. Part of this was due to the help of Count Pallavicini, who awarded Mozart with a golden cross. It was a gift from the Order of the Golden Spur, an organization that allowed certain people access to the Vatican and the Catholic Pope's chambers. This was a pretty big deal! He was given a title, and was now called Signor Cavaliere Mozart (*signor* meaning *sir*), despite only being a child.

In the town of Bologna, Mozart auditioned for the group called *Accademia Filarmonica* - what we might call the *Philharmonic Academy. Philharmonic* describes something that is devoted to music, mainly orchestras. For his audition, he was to sit in a room, working with one short sentence and turning it into a four-part song (this was the type of music that was often used in churches). Mozart took this as a fun challenge. He shocked the members of the *Accademia Filarmonica* when he had written the song in under thirty minutes.

Meanwhile, Mozart had been hard at work on an Italian opera (after all, he was in Italy—it was the perfect time!). His job was to write music to a story. The story was called

Mitridate, Re di Ponto. It hit theaters when he was fourteen years old, in the year 1770. Mozart himself conducted the orchestra that performed at the show.

To say that people loved it is an understatement. Obviously, people knew that the famous boy Mozart was working on the opera. At the end of the performance, they cried out, "*Evviva il maestro!*" From Italian, this translates as, "*Long live the conductor!*" As Mozart took his bows, he was truly happy. Clearly, so was his father Leopold. It seems like all of the pressures and sickness had finally been worth it.

Even though Italy seemed like the best place to be, both Leopold and Mozart decided that they should return to Salzburg. Leopold needed to get back to his job, and Mozart needed a quiet place where he could continue composing. And so they said goodbye to Italy, which stood as one of Mozart's favorite places.

Chapter 3: Mozart Roams Europe

Leopold Mozart was in for a shock when he returned to Salzburg. While he expected to get a raise and a promotion in the Court of Salzburg because of how Mozart had made their family name famous, instead he figured out that the Archbishop of Salzburg had died, and the new one in his place was not a fan of Austrian musicians. Leopold was allowed to keep his job, though, and Wolfgang Amadeus Mozart was appointed to the position of Concert Master.

The Archbishop of Salzburg made many demands of Mozart, requiring symphonies and songs and this and that, and all for a very disappointing paycheck. Mozart never became bored with his work, but it just was not the same as Italy.

He enjoyed Salzburg, though. Even though he was sixteen years old now, he had spent very little time in his hometown, since more than half of his life had already been spent touring Europe. During the next four years that he spent there, Mozart flirted with many girls, but never engaging in any serious relationships. He was far too busy for any of that. The Archbishop's requests filled up Mozart's schedule.

Leopold was disappointed. He knew that his son had so much more potential than sitting around in Salzburg as the "prisoner" of the Archbishop. Even Mozart was itching to get out of the city. But how? They would have to confront the Archbishop and ask to leave.

Mozart and Leopold approached the new Archbishop, who was offended. He said that Mozart could leave, but Leopold needed to stay. While this was frustrating, Leopold accepted it. But he still wanted someone to go with Mozart, so that his son would not be alone. They decided that Mozart's mother, whom they called Frau Mozart, should attend him in his next tour around Europe, while Leopold would guide him through written letters.

Mozart and his mother traveled to the city of Mannheim, Germany, where they came into contact with the Weber family. The patriarch of the family, Fridolin Weber, was a musician and suffering from financial troubles. His eighteen-year old daughter Aloysia was an opera singer, and her voice enchanted Mozart (along with her stunning beauty). Instantly Mozart felt bad for them. For one, he loved music and he hated to see a struggling musical family. Secondly, Fridolin Weber was living under a horribly rude boss, just as his father Leopold lived under the Archbishop of Salzburg.

In a letter to his father, Mozart wrote the following:

"I am so fond of this unfortunate family that my dearest wish would be to make them happy, and perhaps I may actually be able to do so. My advice is that they should go to

Italy. Therefore I want to ask you to write to our good friends there, the sooner the better, and find out how much, and what is the most, they pay a prima donna [*a prima donna is the principal female singer of an opera; he was referring to Aloysia Weber*] in Verona. As to Aloysia's singing, I would stake my life that she will bring me fame. Even in so short a time she has profited by my instruction. [. . .] If our plan succeeds, we—Herr Weber, his two daughters and I—will do ourselves the honor of spending a fortnight with my dear Papa and my dear sister en route. My sister will find a friend and comrade in Fräulein Weber, for her reputation here is like my sister's in Salzburg, her father's like my father's, and the standing of the whole family like that of the family of Mozart. I shall be glad to come to Salzburg with them, if only that you may hear Aloysia sing. She sings my arias superbly. I beg you to do your best to get us to Italy. You know my greatest desire—to write operas."

It may not have been immediately clear to Leopold that Mozart was head-over-heels in love with Aloysia Weber, and he was willing to stake everything for her. Before his father could even reply, Mozart quickly sent another letter to his father, describing how it is better how people to marry for love and not for money. His father, considering all of the financial problems that they been enduring, was obviously not too happy with his son.

The following is an excerpt from Leopold's ten-page response to his son:

"It depends solely on you whether you leave this world having been captured by some petticoat, bedded on straw, and penned-in with an attic full of starving children. Name me one great composer who would deign to take so foolish a step! Off with you to Paris! Find your place among the great."

Because of the level of support that Leopold lent his son, Mozart could not disobey his orders. Leopold had been there for Mozart through thick and thin, taking care of him at every instance on their tour around Europe. No matte what the lovesick Mozart wanted, he needed to leave the Webers behind. Aloysia especially was sad to see him go.

Paris was not the same city that Mozart had remembered. He was no longer a child, so his talent did not inspire incredible wonder. Now, he was just a talented piano player and composer trying to make his way around a world that seemed way too big. People were rude to him and they rejected him at every corner. He realized how difficult it was to arrange performances and meetings with Parisian aristocrats without his father there. His father had always been the best agent.

But even the man who had helped them before, Melchior Grimm, was unforgiving. Like the city, he had changed and was no longer enchanted with Mozart's talent. Grimm had moved up the social ladder and looked down upon Mozart.

During this time period, musicians were often looked upon as servants. All they did was provide entertainment for people who had the money to pay for it. This is something that has changed over time. Before, rich people paid musicians to play for them, and the musicians received enough money to get by. Now that music can be purchased on CDs, iPhones, computers, and more, musicians get paid much more money. Before the invention of recordings, a musician had to be there *in person* to play the song—or sell their sheet music. Try to imagine hiring the Beatles or Macklemore to come play for you in your house—it would be pretty expensive!

Below is a letter that Mozart wrote to his father, about his performance for the Duchesse de Chabot, an aristocrat in France:

> "So I presented myself. On my arrival I was made to wait half an hour in a great ice-cold, unheated room without any fireplace. At length the Duchesse came in, greeted me with the greatest ceremony, begged me to make the best of the clavier [*a clavier is an instrument similar to the harpsichord or the piano*] since it was the only one in order, and asked me to try it.

> "'I am very willing to play something,' I said, 'but momentarily it is impossible, for my hands are numb with the cold,' and I asked her to have me conducted to a room with a fire. '*Oh, oui, Monsieur. Vous avez raison*' was all the answer I received [*This means "Oh, yes, sir. You are right."*]. Thereupon she sat down and began to sketch in company with a party of gentlemen who set in a circle around a large table. There I had the honor of waiting fully an hour. The windows and doors stood open, and not only my hands, but my whole body and my feet were chilled. My head began to ache. There was a profound silence, and I did not know what to do for cold, headache, and boredom. I kept on thinking: If it were not for Grimm I would leave immediately.

> "At last, to be brief, I played on the wretched, miserable piano-forte. Most vexing of all, however, Madame and her gentlemen never ceased their sketching for a moment, so that I had to play to the chairs, tables, and walls. Under these vile conditions, I lost patience. I began to play the *Fischer Variations*, played them half through, and stood up. At once I received a host of compliments. I said, however, what was quite true, namely, that I could not do myself justice with the clavier and should be very glad to choose another day when a better clavier would be available. But she would not consent to let me go; I must wait another half hour until her husband came. He sat beside me and listened with close attention, and I—I forgot cold and headache and in spite of all played the wretched clavier as I do play when I am in the mood. Give me the best clavier in Europe with an audience that understands nothing, desires to understand nothing, and does not feel with me as I play, and I would have no joy in it!"

As you can see, the Duchesse treated Mozart pretty poorly. He felt like he was playing to absolutely no one, and his own discomfort was given no consideration. This goes along with the idea that musicians were seen as no better than servants; considering the raucous applauses that he had received in Italy, you would think that he would be treated with more respect in Paris.

As if this was not enough, his mother fell seriously ill. At first, they did not think it was too threatening. But soon enough she could not raise herself out of bed, and she refused to see any doctor who was French (France and Austria were not the best of friends during this time period). Because of this, she did not get the proper help that she needed.

Mozart sat by her bed and watched her grow frailer with each day. Frau Mozart soon died, when Mozart was twenty-two years old. He had no idea what to do. Where should he bury her? Would there be a funeral? How much did he have to pay? He called on Grimm, who was willing to give him information and help him out.

Frau Mozart was buried in the Saint Eustache Cemetery in Paris, France. If you visit the Saint Eustache Church today, there is a small plaque with her name on it, honoring her life and the powerful and motherly influence she had on her son.

Mozart and his mother had been staying in a two-bedroom apartment; but after the costs of the funeral and the burial, Mozart was completely unable to keep up the cost of rent there. Grimm allowed Mozart to stay at his place. Mozart, however, did not enjoy it. He thought that Grimm was rude and no longer a true friend. Grimm, however, had a completely different idea in mind, and even said so in a letter that he wrote to Leopold:

"Wolfgang is too kindhearted, not active enough, all too easily deceived, too little concerned with the means that can lead him to be crafty, enterprising, and bold. [. . .] In this country the majority of the public do not understand music, and the merit of work is judged only by a very small number of persons. Therefore, *cher maître* [*this means "dear master" in French*], in this city where so many mediocre and even quite wretched musicians enjoy tremendous success, I doubt that your son will be able to cope with conditions. I am explaining the situation to you so bluntly not in order to grieve you, but in order that we may together find the best solution to all these problems."

Most of history's most famous musicians have been famous for one huge reason: they were willing to change the face of music. Johann Sebastian Bach and Ludwig van Beethoven both experimented with music, trying out new techniques and putting new notes together. Mozart had not yet tried this. Instead, he had only ridden on the popularity that his young age and talent had brought him. Now that he was older, he would need to try a different tactic. Essentially, Grimm was completely right about Mozart. He definitely had a soft spot for Mozart, and he wanted Mozart to be successful. But Grimm could not make it happen alone; Mozart would have to do it himself.

Both Grimm and Leopold told Mozart that he should return to Salzburg. Paris was just not the right place for him. Leopold wrote that Mozart would be granted the position of assistant conductor in Salzburg, *and* that Aloysia Weber could live them if he wanted (most historians interpret this as Leopold giving permission for Mozart to propose to Aloysia). But Mozart, for some reason, did not want to leave Paris. In fact, he wanted Aloysia Weber to come to Paris and attempt to jumpstart her musical career there.

Mozart barely had a choice though when Grimm gave him a ticket, fully paid for, back home. Mozart finally gave in and said his farewells, putting Paris behind him. But before he returned to Salzburg, he made a pitstop in the city of Munich, where Aloysia Weber was performing in an opera.

He gave her a gift: a song that he had written for her, called "Populi di Tessaglia." The song is an *aria*, a short piece of music that goes with an opera. The words in the song were romantic and told the story of his love for her. Aloysia, however, did not respond positively. She did not want to be in a relationship with someone who was traveling all the time, especially with her career as a prima donna revving up. Disappointed, Mozart left her behind. He had wanted to be with her for years, and suddenly his hopes and dreams were put down.

Chapter 4: The Return to Vienna

Mozart's return to Salzburg was not an easy one. First, he wanted to bring home his cousin, Maria Thekla, who he had found in his travels. Leopold ordered Maria to come later, but Mozart refused. He wanted to be treated like the man that he now was, no longer a child that needed to obey his father's every command. Despite the friction between Mozart and Leopold, however, his family was overjoyed to see him return to Salzburg. Both Leopold and Nannerl were in tears. This was the first time they had seen Mozart since Frau Mozart had died.

But quite soon upon his return to Salzburg, he was commissioned by the city of Munich, Germany to write music for an opera called *Idomeneo, King of Crete*. The opera comes from a story that was often told in the city of Troy, in the ancient Greek and Roman world. For Mozart, this was a big deal. The other operas he had worked on had been lesser works; they were not nearly so popular and recognized, so Mozart saw a real challenge in this project.

He wanted to write the music in Munich, so he left Salzburg rather quickly. The music writing was slow going. He spent day and night working on the songs, but to write music to this story was indeed intimidating. It was a challenge, but Mozart was more than ready to take it on. He wanted his father's advice, though. Like an author that asks a fellow author to look at his book, it is often common for musicians to ask their fellow musicians to examine their music, check it for any mistakes, and offer any recommendations or improvements.

If you want to know one of the examples of Leopold's suggestions to his son, here is something he wrote in a letter:

"See that you keep the whole orchestra in good humor by flattering them; keep every single one of them well-disposed toward you by praise. For I know your style; it requires the highest degree of incessant concentration from all the players, and it is no easy task to keep an entire orchestra tensed to such a pitch and working so hard for at least three hours. Every one of them, even the worst violinist, is touched by direct praise tête à tête [*this phrase represents a conversation between two people; Leopold is saying that everyone likes to be congratulated in person*], and will therefore work with more eagerness and attention. A gesture of this sort costs you nothing but a few words."

While this suggestion has nothing to do with the actual music that Mozart wrote, Leopold stresses the very important relationship between the conductor and the musician. If Mozart did not make his musicians feel good about themselves, their confidence might drop and the whole performance of the opera could have been a wreck.

When the opera opened in Munich, however, everything went according to plan. Mozart was only twenty-five years old, yet it was one of the best musical operas the world had ever seen. It was one of Mozart's great successes, and one that was seen by hundreds of people in Munich.

After the performance of the opera, Mozart received an exciting letter. The Archbishop of Salzburg was traveling to Vienna, and he wanted Mozart there with him to perform. This excited Mozart; sure, the Archbishop was not the nicest person, but Mozart had loved Vienna, and he would have the opportunity to see the Weber family, who was staying there.

But his happiness was soon defeated when he learned that the Archbishop had a long list of rules in mind. Firstly, Mozart was not allowed to live on his own. He needed to stay with the Archbishop. He was not allowed to sit with the higher-ups, but instead with the servants (Mozart saw this as an insult to his honor; despite the fact that musicians were seen as servants, Mozart saw himself as much grander and respectable than this). He was not allowed to perform for *anyone else*, unless the Archbishop gave prior permission, and he was certainly not allowed to enter the room of any higher-up without first being allowed in by a servant.

While the last rule may seem reasonable, remember that Mozart was granted membership in the Order of the Golden Spur, and he was allowed even into the Pope's chambers. The fact that he was now so suddenly restrained made Mozart furious.

Mozart, ever the rebel, did not listen to the Archbishop. If he did not want to perform for the Archbishop, he did not show up. He performed for whoever he wanted to, often leaving the house to meet other Viennese aristocrats. He found their company enjoyable—certainly more enjoyable than that of the Archbishop of Salzburg.

The Archbishop, of course, was not too happy about this. When he stated that they were all returning to Salzburg, and that Mozart was coming too, whether he liked it or not, Mozart flatly refused. The Archbishop shouted at him and dismissed him from service.

On one hand, this made Mozart happy. On the other, he was out of his main job. Without enough money to properly find a place to live, he asked the Webers for a chance to stay with them. They immediately agreed, and Mozart found himself in their house.

In order to gather a steady source of income, Mozart took on some students. If money was not that great in the performance business (which it was not), he could tutor some up-and-coming musicians! He taught several, and the Princess of Württemberg even showed an interest. The Princess was a member of the royal family, and Mozart's paycheck would have been very thick if he had landed this job. The Emperor of Austria, however, went with another teacher.

The other teacher was named Antonio Salieri, an Italian native to the city of Legnano. Although he did not know it at the time, Mozart and Salieri would soon become rivals.

For now, though, Mozart was merely frustrated that the job opportunity was stolen from him.

Speaking of enemies, you can probably guess that Mozart was good at making them. He was rebellious and stubborn, and very outspoken when it came to his fellow musicians' work. He was not afraid to tell someone that he just did not like their music. But beyond the harsh criticism, he was rude and sarcastic. Sure, his music was great, but many people thought that Mozart was a spoiled brat.

Much like many of the spoiled and bratty celebrities of today, the people of Vienna loved to whisper and rumor about who Mozart was in love with. Mozart himself had no time to even think about marriage—but it was generally thought that Mozart was in love with Constanze, Aloysia Weber's younger sister. Perhaps he considered marriage from time to time, but never seriously; but just being in love was a completely different story.

Take a look at this letter than Mozart wrote to his father, and try to determine things for yourself:

> "Now then, who is the object of my love? Do not be alarmed by this. Certainly not a Weber? Yes, a Weber, but not Josepha, not Sophie, but Constanze, the middle one. . . . She is the martyr among them, and for that very reason perhaps the most sweet natured, the cleverest, and in a word, the best among them. She takes care of everything in the house, and yet they blame her for doing nothing right. Oh, dearest Father, I could write pages if I were to describe to you all the scenes that have happened to us both in that house. She is not ugly, but one could not call her a beauty. Her whole beauty consists in dark eyes and graceful figure. She is not witty, but has enough sound common sense to enable her to fulfill her duties as a wife and mother. She is not inclined to extravagance. That is an altogether false accusation. On the contrary, she is accustomed to going about poorly dressed. For what little the mother has been able to do for her children has been done for the other two, never for Constanze. It is true that she would like to be neatly dressed, but she does not care for the latest fashion. And most al[l] the clothes a woman needs she is able to make for herself. She also does her own hair every day, is a good housekeeper, and has the kindest heart in the world.

> "I love her and she loves me—with all our hearts. How could I wish myself a better wife! One thing more I must tell you, which that I was not in love with her at the time of my resignation. It was born of her tender care when I lodged in their house. Accordingly I wish for nothing else but a small, secure income (of which, thank God, I have well-founded hope), and then I shall ask your blessing to save this poor girl—and myself with her—and I think I may say, make us all happy."

After reading a letter like this, it is quite obvious that Mozart was in love with the girl, but marriage was another idea entirely. For now, he wanted to make himself an established musician in Vienna and gain a consistent audience. But in terms of creating a long-term relationship with Constanze Weber, his hopes were pretty slim. Her guardian did not want her reputation to be tarnished by eventually marrying a rude musician like Mozart.

Constanze had other plans in mind, though. Her family life had been miserable as of late. She was mistreated by her mother, whom they called Frau Mozart, given very little respect, and paid little attention to. She fled home, moved in with a friend, and soon after moved in with none other than Wolfgang Mozart.

The Webers were shocked. As much as they had liked Mozart, they saw this as a rebellious and unforgiving act. They demanded that Constanze return to them immediately, or else they would have the police forcibly return her to the Weber household. Mozart was now torn. Did he harbor the girl that he loved and risk a run-in with the Viennese police, or did he give Constanze up against her will?

He wrote a letter to a friend, a Baroness in Vienna, asking for advice. In the letter, he said:

> "The maid told me of a prospect which, while I scarcely believe it could come to pass, since it would amount to dishonor for the entire family, yet may be possible in the light of Frau Weber's stupidity, and therefore worries me [*the "prospect" in this situation in Frau Weber's likelihood of calling the police on Mozart*]. Are the police here in Vienna allowed to walk right into my house? Perhaps it is only a trick to make her return home. But if the threat could be carried out, then I know no finer way to counter it than to marry Constanze tomorrow morning—even today, if that were possible. For I should not like to expose my beloved to such a disgrace, and nothing could be done to her if she were my wife. One thing more: the Webers have sent for Thorwarth [*Thorwarth is Constance's official guardian*]. I ask your Ladyship for your kind advice, and to lend a helping hand to us poor creatures. You can reach me any time at home. I write this in the greatest haste. Constanze does not yet know anything of this."

You can see how desperate Mozart was, and how closely he was backed into a corner. What was he supposed to do? Only a marriage between him and Constanze would solve the problem. If Constanze was his wife, her family would be unable to take her away from him by law.

Mozart and Constanze married on August 4th, 1782. Frau Weber was obviously not too happy about this, yet she still attended the wedding. After all, it was not she that disagreed to the marriage. Thorwarth, Constanze's guardian, was the most opposed. For a situation that had started so poorly, Mozart was ecstatic at the marriage. He loved Constanze, and even if the circumstances of their marriage weren't exactly ideal, he was still happy to have her.

Chapter 5: Uphill and Downhill

Married life for Mozart went better than expected. Despite the fact that their marriage was born out of some family trouble, they were very content together. They loved attending concerts and operas and balls and parties, and finances were not too big of a deal. Constanze was perhaps the perfect partner for Mozart. She knew that, as a musician, he needed his space in order to write. When he needed her opinion, she was more than happy to help him and give him constructive criticism. Besides that, they loved spending time together. They were two peas in a pod.

In addition to attending his marriage with Constanze, life in Vienna was busy. He still taught students, he was still composing music (which the people loved), and he still sat at dinners held by high aristocrats. This was Mozart's way of being his own agent; if he wanted to perform for the rich, he needed to know them and become their friends. He did this by making connections in the higher circles of Viennese society, and it was successful.

A year after Constanze and Mozart married, Constanze gave birth to a beautiful baby boy. They named him Raimund Leopold: *Raimund*, after the child's godfather, the Baron Raimund Weltzar, who had allowed Constanze and Mozart to stay at his house once, and who was a good friend to them; and *Leopold*, after Mozart's father.

After the birth of the child, Constanze and Mozart traveled to Salzburg (although they left Raimund Leopold with a friend in Vienna), so that they could visit Mozart's family. The atmosphere in the Mozart household was not very friendly. For one thing, Leopold had never given Mozart permission to marry Constanze. Secondly, Leopold was insulted that his own name came second in Mozart's child's name. The visit was unpleasant and uncomfortable, and the city did not seem the same to Mozart. He had lost touch with a lot of his friends, and Constanze found no warmth in the home of her in-laws.

When they left after a three-month stay, Mozart could not have known that it would be the last time he ever saw Salzburg.

After a miserable trip, Constance and Mozart returned to Vienna to hear some miserable news. While they were away, Raimund Leopold had died of sickness. This was a terrible blow for the new parents, who had spent barely any time with their son. It was common for children to die early from sickness, but that does mean that it was any less sad for Mozart. Both he and Constanze mourned for their child.

Despite the fact that their visit to Salzburg had gone horribly wrong, Leopold understood what the two parents were going through, having lost children himself. He decided he would come stay with them in Vienna, where he could watch his son in his musical life.

In Vienna, Leopold met Joseph Haydn, another one of the most famous musicians of all time. Haydn told Leopold that "your son is the greatest composer I know in person or by name. He has taste, moreover, the most thorough knowledge of composition."

Leopold was also happy to see that Mozart and Constanze had their second child, whom they yet again did not name after him. Instead they named the child Karl Thomas. When life seemed to pick up for Mozart after the death of his son, he realized that it was becoming harder and harder to find musical jobs. Many of the Viennese aristocrats were more interested in younger up-and-coming musicians, while Mozart had already found himself a comfortable niche that was quickly wearing away.

The opera that he had been working on for awhile, *Le nozze di Figaro*, had very little success in Vienna. His clients were uninterested in his work. His third son lived less than a month. He asked his father to take care of Karl Thomas for a while, but was flatly rejected. With all of these factors swirling around in his head, Mozart became hopelessly depressed.

When things seemed their absolute worst, he heard news that a performance in Prague of *Le nozze di Figaro* had been well received—and they wanted Mozart to come and conduct a concert! Obviously, he left right away. No one had desperately wanted his attention for months, and here was his chance! After the concert and the glorious reception, however, things went downhill. No matter how great Mozart's experience in Prague was, his return to Vienna was depressing. Money was a constant problem now. His father was ill in Salzburg. He sometimes found it troubling to keep composing music with so many problems in his life.

And then something very interesting happened. As he sat in his house, he was told that someone had arrived to see him: a sixteen-year old boy by the name of Ludwig van Beethoven. Mozart had heard of Beethoven, a young German prodigy. Beethoven, like himself, had started playing the piano just a few years after he was born. But Mozart had some doubts. Sure, people around Europe had been discussing Beethoven—but was he really all that?

He allowed the boy into his house and invited him into the piano parlor. Mozart asked Beethoven to sit at the piano and play something. Beethoven eagerly started to play something that Mozart had written years ago—but Mozart stopped him, and asked him to play something that he had written himself. Unless Beethoven played something original, how could Mozart properly judge his composing and playing abilities? Beethoven nodded and continued.

Mozart was stunned. He stood up when the boy was done and strode into the next room to get Constanze. He told her that Beethoven was simply amazing, and that he would be honored to have Beethoven as one of his students—which is one of the reasons that Beethoven traveled from Bonn, Germany to Vienna, Austria.

People had already been suggesting that perhaps one day Beethoven would grow to be the next Mozart—and Mozart wanted to make that dream become a reality. But Beethoven was not able to stick around for long. His mother was seriously ill, and he needed to leave Austria. Sadly, this would be the only time that Mozart and Beethoven would meet. The next time that Beethoven would return to Austria, Mozart would be dead.

Chapter 6: Money Troubles

But for now, Mozart had a good amount of time to live his life. The same could not be said for his father, who sadly passed away on May 28, 1787, when Mozart was thirty-one years old. You would think that Mozart might be sad over the death of Leopold, but it was not a huge event in his life. His relationship with his father had been a rather difficult one. Both men had been consistently stubborn, and Mozart was always a rebellious son.

After his father's death, Mozart wrote one of his more famous pieces, known as *Eine kleine Nachtmusik*. It is a piece of music that has been used in many movies and television shows to indicate fancy parties or gala events of significant wealth. Many orchestras across the world, especially in middle schools and high schools, play this song to introduce the students to the world of classical music. You can find this song online and listen to it, to get an idea of perhaps Mozart's most recognizable song.

Besides working on that, he was hard at work on an opera that consumed most of his time. He still tried to maintain his connections in the higher circles of Viennese wealth, while taking care of his wife and child. How did he maintain such a busy schedule?

In a letter, Mozart once wrote:

> "I really cannot say much on this subject, for I myself cannot account for it. When I am, as it were, quite alone, and in a good humor—say, traveling in a carriage, or walking after a good meal—or during the night when I cannot sleep, it is on such occasions that my ideas flow best and most abundantly. *Whence* and *how* they come, I don't know; nor can I force them. I remember those ideas that I like, and am accustomed, as I have been told, to hum them to myself. If I continue in this way, it soon occurs to me how I may turn this or that morsel to account so as to make a good dish of it, that is to say, agreeable to the rules of counterpoint, to the peculiarities of various instruments, and so forth. All this fires my soul and, provided I am not disturbed, my subject enlarges itself, becomes organized and defined, and the whole, though it be long, stands almost complete and finished in my mind, so that I can survey it, like a fine picture, or a beautiful statue, at a glance. In my imagination I don't hear the parts *successively*, but I hear them as it were*, gleich alles zusammen* [*this phrase means "all together"*], all at once. What a delight this is! All this inventing, the creating, takes place in a lively pleasant dream. What has thus been created I do not easily forget, and this is perhaps the best gift I have to thank my Divine Maker for."

This entry shows Mozart's thought process when he writes music, which is important for understanding how he lived his daily life. He was a genius, even if his music was not exactly celebrated everywhere during his life. Even if he did come upon very hard financial times, his music was still innovative and creative.

He had been staying in Prague to work on the opera *Don Giovanni*, which was received even better than *La nozze di Figaro* was. This made him happy, especially it meant the opera had come to an end. Working through all of the opera's music had been especially trying for Mozart, who had been feeling rather under the weather lately. He was glad to say goodbye to Prague, and say hello once again to Vienna.

But upon his return, he received quite an unexpected letter. The King of Prussia, an old country in Europe that no longer exists, wanted Mozart to come and play for him, especially after the excellent reception of *Don Giovanni*. How could he turn down such an excellent opportunity? He knew that he would not be able to take Constanze with him, since she would need to stay home and take care of their six-year old son Karl Thomas.

Before he left, he decided that he would write her a sad poem; he would miss his wife dearly while he was away.

> *"Now that for Berlin I am departing*
> *I hope to win much fame and honor there.*
> *But endless praises are not worth a farthing*
> *If you, my wife, do not add your share.*
> *When we two meet again, oh what embraces.*
> *But now the tears are streaming down our faces.*
> *Our hearts will burst, so sad now is our plight."*

The trip was brief and not as successful as he had hoped; King Frederick Wilhelm II of Prussia was rather dull company, and the music he wanted Mozart to play was very simple and easy. Upon his return home, he found Constanze in a terrible state. She was pregnant yet again, but the pregnancy had made her ill. While he never left her bedside, he was still burdened with money troubles. He needed to pay her medical bills, and he could barely compose music with so much on his mind.

Mozart knew that he needed help—quickly. Recently, he had been made a brother of the Masonic Lodge, an organization of Freemasons that was very popular in Mozart's time, and still exists today. He wrote to one of his fellow Freemasons:

> "Oh God. I think I need not tell you again that I have been prevented from earning anything by Constanze's unfortunate illness; but I must mention that despite my miserable condition I decided to give a subscription concert at home, so that I could at least meet my great day-by-day expenses. But even this failed me. Fate is so against me (though only in Vienna) that I cannot earn any money no matter what I do. I sent around a list soliciting subscriptions for the concert a fortnight ago, and the only name upon it is that of Baron Swietan."

While Mozart had once found only warmth and happiness in the city of Vienna, he found it quite changed. All of his troubles were here. Constanze made it through her illness, just barely, and Mozart began to compose music again, while also taking on new students to make extra money. It still just did not seem like enough, however.

Chapter 7: The Death and Legacy of Mozart

One day, Mozart received a very strange visitor on his doorstep. The man was tall and looked like a skeleton, wearing nothing but gray. He left a letter for Mozart and left, without speaking a word. Frightened, Mozart opened the letter. It ordered him to compose a requiem, which is a type of song that is used to honor the dead at a church service. The letter told Mozart that he was not allowed to try to figure out who wanted the song composed, and that he was to speak to *no one* about this except the messenger, who Mozart called the "man in gray."

Mozart, a superstitious man, saw this as Fate telling him that his death was soon upon him, that he was writing his own requiem, a song that honored his own death. He met the Man in Gray one more time, and they agreed to the terms of the requiem and how much Mozart would be paid in exchange for the music.

If you can imagine what was going through Mozart's mind after this strange visitation, you will probably guess that he was scared out of his wits and that he did not know how to exactly start such a song. In a letter to one of his friends, Da Ponte, Mozart said:

"I am confused; I can think only with difficulty, and cannot free my mind of the image of the Unknown. I constantly see him before me, he pleads with me, urges me on and impatiently demands the work from me. I am continuing with it because composing is less tiring than doing nothing. Besides, I have nothing to fear. I can feel from my present state that the hour is striking. I am on the point of expiring. My end has come before I was able to profit by my talent. And yet life has been so beautiful; my career began under such fortunate auspices. But no one can change his fate. No one can count his days; one must resign oneself. What Providence determines will be done. I close now. Before me lies my swan song. I must not leave it unfinished."

Mozart truly saw this song as the end of his days. He called the song nothing more then *Requiem*, and it was one of the most beautiful and haunting songs ever written. You can find it on the Internet and listen to it in its entirety (although the song stands at nearly one hour long). While the song is not slow all the time, it is dramatic and frightening. It definitely represents the state of Mozart's mind at the time. With his sickness looming over him like a sword, he thought that he was composing himself into his own grave.

At the same time that he composed *Requiem*, he worked on a piece called *The Magic Flute* for an opera performance. This piece is much more upbeat and entertaining, fit for an opera. It stands at a much longer length, about two hours.

He finished both of the works very content, and then even went on to write two more pieces, one of them being a *Concerto for Clarinet*, one of the most popular pieces for clarinet players around the world. A larger orchestra accompanies the clarinet, a solo instrument in the piece. The *Concerto for Clarinet* is one of his most popular pieces of music. He conducted the concerto on November 18, 1791, not knowing that this would be his final performance.

Soon after the concert, he fell dangerously sick. He was cold all the time and he kept on vomiting. Constanze refused to leave his bedside, and the doctors said there was not much that would be able to save him.

He died soon after, at 12:05 on the fifth of December, 1791.

His own wife was unable to attend his funeral, because she was too sick. Unlike the funerals of the great composers that came before and after him, only five people came to honor Mozart: two of his students, a family friend, his rival Salieri, and a local manager of a tavern. For a man who left us with such great music, this is very sad to hear. The funeral was cheap and not much of a sight. He was buried in a coffin made of inexpensive, unpainted planks of wood.

It is a common theory that Mozart was perhaps murdered. By who? Some say Antonio Salieri, who had constantly competed with Mozart throughout their lifetimes. Upon hearing of Mozart's death, Salieri said that "It is indeed a pity to lose such a genius, but his death is a good thing for us. If he had lived longer not a soul would have given us a bit of bread for *our* compositions."

Clearly, Salieri was jealous, but beyond that, historians find no reason to suspect Salieri of anything. Most historians believe it was the combination of stress, sickness, and winter that finally got to Mozart.

So what is Mozart's legacy? Did he give the world anything else besides music?

Often, he is remembered as a down-on-his-luck musician. For such a talented man, he received so little in life: so little respect, so little payment. Today, he is celebrated as a genius. Even if people loved his music while he was alive, they did not show it too well. Now that we can look back on the age of classical music, we can see how much he taught the musicians that came after him.

Ludwig van Beethoven, one of the most celebrated musicians of all time, often cited Mozart as his principal inspiration. Beethoven was not the only one. Across the world today, Mozart is played in schools and concert halls. Throughout his life he wrote hundreds of pieces of music; it would take years to learn them all, much less learn to play them proficiently.

His busy life started early, going on tour when he was only five years old. But the child-celebrity status could not help him later on in life, despite his brilliance. Out of all the music that was produced in the classical era, perhaps his is the most memorable. Mozart was an absolute genius, and he will always be remembered as one.

Made in the USA
Lexington, KY
31 March 2016